The Gift Of Imagining

by
Rosemary Arthur

With illustrations by:

Gillian Rose Peace
A.H. Rock
Rosemary Arthur

Gills Verse Publications
11 Lupin Works, Worcester Road,
Kidderminster, Worc's, England.
DY10 1JR.

British Library Cataloguing-in-Publication Data.

*A book should be the key
that opens the
greatest gift of all,
imagination.*

By the same author:

**Aspects of Autumn
Miscellany
The Halcyon Days
Swansong
Swansong and Solo Verses**

ISBN 0 9511898 9 1
Printed in England by Sales Print Design Ltd.

THE GIFT OF IMAGINATION

CONTENTS

STRANGE QUARTET

There were four who put their mark upon my being
shaped my character with their influence
and formed a strange quartet;
first there was my Father, a self made man
who gave and kept his word with just a handshake
who had no time for fools, could spot a fake
a mile away, but had a certain way with animals, the knack
that made them sense he was the leader of the pack.

My Mother's name was Rose, and she was aptly named,
softly curved, sweet scented but with a sharp
and piercing thorn if harshly treated;
I see her in her later years, relaxing in the afternoons
serenely dressed in crepe-de-chine, and Father said
her ankles were as fine as any thoroughbred.

Aunt Mary was the widow of a miner wounded in
the Battle of The Somme, she has now been dead
for many years, but I remember her home had the aroma
of crisp starched linen and new baked bread,
and she created beauty from bare necessity
and covered the privy at the bottom of her garden
with a rambling rose, and saw only the flowers,
and was content to doze in her chair, rocking to and fro
as she listened to the voice of Perry Como.

My lover was as wholesome as a jar of honey,
pure nectar spiced with acid, with all the lure
of nature's guile, white teeth in a sunburnt face
and an angel's smile - but his temper was as awesome
as a clap of thunder and if I was afraid he would
sink to his knees and cradle me in loving arms
as strong as Hercules.

The members of this unique quartet are not easy to forget
when memory stirs the strings, for they taught me
many things, honesty, courage and determination,
and maybe the greatest gift of all - imagination.

WORD PICTURES

They say - there is no original thought,
no original experience - it has all been done before,
said before, told before - and maybe so,
but differently, and not by me.
I take a subject, analyse it and describe it,
create a picture not with paint and canvas
but in my mind with words,
to stir memories, start fantasies - triggering
imagination.

I am no Michelangelo, but I have come to know
my word pictures strike a chord,
and make folk laugh or make folk cry, or
set them wondering why life is more strange
than any story book
and if you just look around and see
you too will find pictures and memories stored
in your mind - so take them out and dust them down,
treasure them for they are the foundations
on which to build your life, maybe
the start of a better way to possess
that elusive quality we call happiness.

PIGEON POST

Photo: Gillian Rose Peace

FOOTPRINTS LEAVING

When we go, we leave tangible marks behind,
shoes creased by repeated strides,
indentations on a well-loved chair,
gloved fingers wrinkled by a mobile hand
and lingering perfume in the air,
clothes moulded to a certain form,
the handles of our garden tools
from endless chores worn smooth and warm,
books, not virgin clean, neglected,
but handled, brought to life by being read.

The words we speak, the deeds we do,
all create a world apart -
fleeting impressions on a gigantic chart as time
the relentless encroaching tide dissolves the chain,
obliterating everything, but recollections still remain -
after I have gone I hope there will be
an echo of shared laughter
as my memory.

PEARLS

The pearls lay on a purple velvet bed
luminous as the eyes of a woman who is loved,
evoking all the wisdom of age,
and the pure innocence of a new-born babe -
pearls with the sheen of a mayfly's iridescent wing,
coloured and warmed by the milk of kindness.

When men desire to enslave their beloved
they encircle her neck with a precious chain
that glows and comes alive against her skin,
created, as many lasting things of beauty are,
out of torment, born of pain -
pearls of wisdom and of truth,
and for some,
pearls for tears.

FLOWER POWER

Delight me with flowers in Springtime, with
primroses and cowslips, tall blue iris and bright waxy tulips,
bring me a bunch of freesias steeped in faint perfume
and all the other early flowers that bloom.

Enchant me with flowers in Summer when the days are
long and sunny and gardens overflow with colour
and the bees are full of honey,
bring me soft blue scabious and columbines and roses,
sweet scented pinks arranged in charming posies,
old-fashioned sweet williams and canterbury bells
and wide-eyed daisies casting spells that
transport me back to childhood days with
memories of sweet meadow bouquets.

And for just once in my life, make me a first-night star,
and fill my room with every kind of bloom,
entice me with the spice scent of pink carnations,
dazzle me with bold lilies of Enchantment, amber and gold,
let baskets overflow with cascading flowers to delight
my eyes, and the perfume, potent as any drug
will waft me to Paradise.

In Winter, when the skies are grey and cold,
fill my arms with daffodils in all shades of gold,
let their trumpets blare your love, but whisper it
to me softly with pale shy primroses,
and to assure me you have no regrets,
in the morning bring me violets.

ROSEMARY'S TAPESTRY GARDEN

Photo: Rosemary Arthur

A DISTANT NIGHTINGALE

How tantilizing is the dream
just beyond our comprehension,
as the choicest fruit on the topmost bough -
just out of reach.

To almost catch a rainbow
as it skips over the fields and hedgerows
like a vast Jack-o-Lantern.

To glimpse a mirage of the far pavilions,
beautiful and unattainable;
see love grow from a stranger's smile
and watch it die from close proximity.

To stand in perfect peace
listening to the quiet sound of water
and in the still pale dusk to hear the sweet song
of a distant nightingale.

LACED WITH HONEY

The written word, studied, measured for effect
can give a picture false as a maiden's modesty;
passion deleted, anger controlled,
channelled into considered intelligence -
an illusion of wisdom or mannered courtesy -
letters on a page with no sign of youth or age,
or if the voice sounds soothing to the ear
or how the writer looks;
mere words can enchant the romantic reader
to form a being with no faults,
not seeing the basket filled with discarded thoughts,
a mind searching for a honeyed phrase.

The spoken word is a different story,
tongue-tied reality, hesitant, often stupid;
or spontaneous with feigned affinity
leading then to dillusion
for the tongue is rarely subtle as the pen.

It takes the brave to risk a meeting
a brief glance, a discreet fleeting, for
reality can break the spell of fantasy
created by easy flowing words
so sweetly laced with honey.

FOOD FOR THOUGHT

My mind is like a great big cooking pot -
a wholesome stew, comforting and hot,
crammed full of every kind of flavour, texture, colour,
blending and mellowing as it simmers on the hob;
the stock is commonsense, with the meat of knowledge,
onions for wisdom, carrots for vision,
patience for flavour, and with the pain of salt and
curiosity of seasoning to give it body
and to give it bite,
stirred well by memory and ladled with experience.

Sometimes my mind is more like a rich celebration cake,
with time the basic flour, happiness the fruit,
blended with the butter of compassion
and the eggs of hope,
add laughter for the sugar, impatience for the yeast
and intelligence to give it flavour,
mixed in a bowl marked anticipation,
and baked slowly to perfection in the oven
of maturity,
iced with fantasy and decorated with
the joy of living.

THE MASTERPIECE

They told me the picture was by an Impressionist -
it certainly made an impression on me,
colours all blurred and indistinct,
like the world looks to me after a night
when wine flows too freely
and I awake with someone else's head.

I think I could paint a picture one day
if I had a canvas and some paint
and my head stops throbbing -
why not use the walls in Lucinda's room?
they look so bare with all the posters gone -
it could encircle the wall like Monet's waterlilies.

I feel sure it will be a masterpiece -
I'll start it right away;
I'll go out and buy the brushes and some paint
when my head stops throbbing
and my hands stop shaking -
maybe not today,
perhaps tomorrow,
or the day after.

THE LADY IN THE PARK

The Park was a fascinating place,
with flowers and trees and a large open space
in which once or twice a year there would appear
tents and stalls, and it would host the Village Fete,
and the boy looked forward to this certain date
when clutching his father's hand, he would listen
spellbound to the band, and watch the ladies
in their summer dresses, imagining they were all princesses,
but best of all, he would creep closer to The Hall,
to the private garden with the high stone wall,
and through the trees he would hope to see
a figure in graceful drapery, a lady, pale as a ghost,
demure and shy - he wondered why she was so still;
then he would lose sight of her in the trees
when leaves were swaying in the breeze,
and he would dream of her, and how one day
he would carry her away, when he became a man -
but then, the War began.

The Hall was closed, The Park deserted, no Village Fetes,
just children tempted to climb the iron gates,
and the boy grew up and moved away, all dreams forgotten
until one day when driving through the countryside
he passed the house where his father died,
and went on to The Hall, now neglected and in disrepair -
why had his footsteps led him there? - through the gate
into The Park, beside the lake, so still and dark
to the garden with the high stone wall, and memories all
came flooding back, and he thought of the lady of his
childhood schemes, the focus of his romantic dreams -
he came upon the sight of her, no longer pale and white,
for moss and lichen clothed her in a gown of green,
the Grecian Lady in the sylvan scene;
he smiled and turned away, leaving her all alone,
the lovely lady made of stone, but her image had stayed
with him so long she would always belong
to his memories, for though many years of living
had left their mark, he would often remember
the Lady in The park.

THE LADY
Photo: A. H. Rock

THE TOUCH OF A HAND

She did not wish to go, but neither could
she bear to stay - they say hearts do not break,
but how they ache.

How can you talk to someone with no time to spare,
no time to listen, no time to care -
he never understood, he did not even try -
how could all those dreams just fade and die?
it needs just one to make a move, to show all is not lost
just try to prove that love does not always die
if both can forgive, it need not be goodbye.

She turned to walk away, feeling all was lost,
she could not stay
then she looked back, eyes filled with tears
as memories came back of happier years,
and he said 'Don't go' and took her hand
and promised he would try to understand,
begged her to stay and try again,
and though she could never forget the pain,
she knew she could not leave, she could not
bear to part, for when he touched her hand
it touched her heart.

THE VIGIL

What shall I do when you are gone,
no longer here to share,
you who are my restricted world
my life and my despair -
all passion spent, all dreams are dead
just barren thoughts to fill my head.

I watch you as you sleep and reminisce
of the first 'Hello' the first shy kiss,
and now I see a body but no soul
the passing years demand a heavy toll;
death may strike too soon or drag too late
as the reaper hovers by the gate,
the burden grows more heavy and
patience wears more thin through endless nights
watching dawn begin.

Sometimes I long to be myself and get away
before the nerve ends start to fray,
but how shall I feel when I am freed
from the vigil fate decreed -
free to do some things we had planned,
but you awake, reach for my hand,
and whatever I had hoped to do will have to wait
even for another year, for I realise
my place is here.

A CLEAR WINDOW

When I was young, I was built for speed
and ran full tilt at life, falling headlong
in my wide-eyed eagerness to see the wonders
and the beauty on the way.

As I grew older I walked not ran
slowing to a steady pace as I began to realise
life is not fair
we do not have an equal share of happiness or sorrow;
I loved and lost and loved again, tried to
disguise the pain, for some we lose and some we gain,
and with eyes grown dim with sadness I viewed life
differently as I looked through a window with
a frosted pane.

But now I am content to watch the world go by
and sit in the comfort of an easy chair,
for there is nothing new to me - I have seen it all -
or most of it, and I have learnt that life
is a kind of feast, where laughter is the yeast,
so now my eyes are lightened by good humour
and as Autumn casts its amber shadow,
the view is through a clearer window.

SKYE VIEW
Photo: A. H. Rock

THE BLOOMING OF THE GORSE

In Spring the birds will mate, the sap will rise
and men will gaze with lustful eyes
at girls whose thoughts are often filled
with dreams of bridal gowns, instinct instilled
when the voice of the turtle can be heard
nesting is not only for the birds.

Love follows neither rhyme nor reason
Cupid strikes in every season,
and there is a saying "kissing's out of fashion
when the gorse is out of bloom", but as there is
no end to love and passion country folk
are very wise with a sly humour, for of course,
even in the bleakest winter
there are flowers on the gorse.

FLOWERS OF THE FIELD

Why do we call some plants weeds?
they are only flowers growing from wind-scattered seeds
needing no help from man to stay alive
in spite of everything we do, they still survive
to brighten up the roadside verges as we pass
golden buttercups and dandelions that gild the grass,
for down many a quiet country lane
the weeds are creeping back again, to remind us
of long -gone country meadows and softly flowing streams
recreating an atmosphere of peace, and childhood dreams
where grass is jewelled by many tiny flowers
springing into life after sudden showers.

The old fashioned names lend an added grace,
changing common cow parsley into Queen Anne's lace,
and many old names really please
like ragged robin, ladysmocks and heartsease,
love-in-idleness, traveller's joy and columbine,
harebells, cranesbills and eglantine, and what of
the violets and creamy blossoms of the hawthorn
and the bright scarlet poppies in the corn -
I wonder how many of the modern ills could be healed
if we could pause a while and consider
the flowers of the field.

THE NECKLACE

Love and pain are intermingled in my heart
together with the rain, now he has gone;
we fell in love in softly falling rain
and it became a joke that it followed us
like an over-protective chaperone.

It rained the last time he loved me -
heavy thunder rain that came out of a
perfect summer sky, and sent us laughing
to the shelter of the trees
transformed to glittering chandeliers
by cascading entrapped rainbows, dancing leaf to leaf -
a magical world, ephemeral and timeless,
unreal as Camelot;
and on a five-barred gate,
drops caught and held for a brief moment
brilliant as diamonds.

He told me he would shower me with jewels
when he was rich, and from the topmost bar
he gathered the irradiant drops for a necklace -
we laughed when they burst like bubbles in champagne,
but reality came too soon,
a broken body in a metal tomb;
as I lift my face to the healing touch of rain
numbness dulls the pain -
I cannot sleep, I cannot weep,
my heart is arrid, desolate,
but the sky shed its tears for me
and hung them on the gate;
amid the memories of love and laughter
is a necklace, locked in the fastness of my heart,
a brief remnant of a life apart.

THE STREAM AT MILL POOL
Photo: Rosemary Arthur

TO BE NEEDED

Youth longs for many things
for imagination has powerful wings
to take us to dazzling heights of ambition,
longings and romantic flights,
desiring to be admired and witty
to be beautiful and not merely pretty,
or to be a hero always scoring goals
or an actor playing all the starring roles,
for if you have courage and believe
there is so much you can achieve.

But the years go by so quickly, and most of us
are also-rans, without the ability to make true
the dreamed of plans, but if you have failed
to acquire riches, nor found a talent that enriches,
do not feel a failure and despair
there maybe someone depending on your care,
and if you fear you will leave no mark behind
there may be comfort of a kind
to know that you have not failed, but succeeded
if you are not only loved,
but you are needed.

THE FRAGMENTED HEART

Do not leave me alone in this unfriendly world,
so far from home,
Please God do not let him die so soon;
take my breath and give to him
there is enough for two -
let my fragmented heart beat for us both,
I shall have no need of it
in my isolation.

Allow him to cling to
the slender thread of life
till I am reconciled to separation,
and in your wisdom
consider a reprieve
to shorten my life sentence
in dark solitude
my private Calvary.

LOVERS WALK

Come walk with me down undiscovered lanes
or in impersonal city streets
where we can stroll, arm through arm,
your hand in mine
and not a soul will know
no one will speculate.

Walk by my side through fields and woods
and I will match you stride for stride,
together we will sing the songs of love
of twenty years ago
and feel as young as we were then.

Soon I will be with you
waiting for the Trans-Atlantic plane
and we shall sit and talk
but shall not say what we would like to say,
but you will know and understand
as I wave until you are but a speck
in the vast eternity of sky -
then I shall turn, and walk
silent and alone
back to my home.

THE EYE OF THE STORM

The hurricane and the typhoon and lashing rain
devastates the earth, causing pain
to all living creatures, most of all to man
but this has been the way since life began,
teaching us to start again
to rebuild our homes and lives and be more fulfilled,
giving us a chance to reshape all things we need
but most of all, we are freed
from former bonds and ties,
with space and vision we need no longer compromise,
and from the chaos we may find a newer, better way
leaving bitterness behind.

At the eye of the storm is the centre that is still,
and for anyone who lends an ear and has the will
to learn, in the midst of the violence
is a kind of peace,
where all the tumult seems to cease,
and if you have the strength to ride the storm
to the all seeing eye, you will have
the wisdom to reason why the stillness
and the peace tells us to reform
for we know then that it is God who is the pivot
in the still eye of the storm.

BIG SPENDER - BLACK COUNTRY HUMOUR

What kind of crisps d'you want, he'd say
or would you like a Mars, or a Kit-Kat?
and I'd settle for that -
its not the food I go for
but the conversation.

Sometimes we go into the country, it's lovely there
the air is so different, and when
money's a bit short, you have to sort-of
be careful -
one day we went to Llandudno, in Wales you know -
in October when prices were low - and
he had a big steak and I had poached salmon
and salad - we went mad that day -
he says we may go back, but it was only two years ago
and we mustn't make a habit of it;
perhaps when we're old we'll have more meals like that
'cos I've been told there's nothing much else to do
then is there?

Give us a kiss and lend us a bob he'll say,
and then I'll have to pay -
it's not that he's really mean, just more keen
on the things that don't cost money,
and it's great when it's sunny,
but we always take a mac.

Sometimes I'm sad, 'cos I don't think we'll ever go
back to Llandudno, so today I think
I'll spend some of my cash and cut a dash
like them in Dynasty -
and have a shandy with the crisps.

THE TREE
Photo: Gillian Rose Peace

IN RETROSPECT

I regret the years between
if only we could have been wise beyond our youth;
we were inseparable, as all young creatures are
growing into love, playing in the endless sunlit days
emotions soaring pavilions high
hit by a dancing blade of laughter,
finding wonder in an uncharted land
of pounding drums in wild cacophony
breaking the fragile shell of innocence -
we briefly held the flowers of paradise
in our careless hands, blossoms that withered
before they bore the fruit, for youth needs to
spread its wings to new horizons, to tread the
distant alien soil and taste the wine on other lips.

The drums are muffled now, the heartstrings muted,
in retrospect I feel we have been truly blessed
to have grown from the wondrous awakening of youth
into the maturity of fulfilment;
the ageing barren tree still feels the sun and rain,
sap rises in the eternal spring
and emerald transforms the hazel eye;
the errant key turns in the lock,
two parts combine to form the perfect whole,
and once more we share the bread and wine of life,
your arms enfold me close in bonds of love,
tender as the dawnlight, blind as the mole;
the velvet night is soft and warm,
the lamp of love is lit and bright,
why should I grieve for years now gone
now you and I once more are one.

YOUR MOVE

The table doesn't fit and neither do the chairs,
and a home is very different not having any stairs,
we realise now that the garage is too small
and how hideous is the fitted cupboard in the hall,
the curtains that we brought are much too short,
and the garden looks so bare though weeds are everywhere;
the dog next door barks all day, and
scared our cat so she ran away - why did you have to say
we were stuck in a groove and it was time to move?

I think of our old home with affection now,
but I mustn't say it would start a row -
I doubt if I'll ever settle here, but if you too regret it,
and are thinking of another move -
forget it!

FORBIDDEN

I often dream of meringues, eclairs and crepe suzette,
gateaux, ice-cream sundaes, chocolate,
treacle tarts and apple turnovers,
light souffles and sweet pavlovas,
stomach drooling, eyes devouring,
the mere temptation's overpowering -
who devised we should be ruled
by calories, not luscious food?

Once more we start a slimming craze,
chicken salads but no mayonnaise,
brown rice like dessicated bones
ensure we are sylphlike clones,
lettuce, cucumber and tomatoes,
apples, grapes and avocados -
colourful as a still life painting -
and as unexciting.

We can feast our eyes but not our body,
keep thoughts pure and celibate,
by turning desire into negation
and only rarely celebrate,
deny temptation in the name of sweetness
and all things taken to excess -
they are as the fruits of Eden,
objects of desire,
but quite forbidden.

RE-UNION

When I die
do not throw my ashes to the wind
or sink them in the sea
nor hide them in a silver casket on the shelf,
but re-unite me with my own true love
who left me sad and lonely,
detached from life as though
I watch myself upon a stage,
standing in the wings
waiting for the final scene.

We were so close in life
in body, thought and mind,
so please be kind,
and mingle my ashes with my love,
scatter them upon his grave,
sow some seeds of Honesty,
and in the Spring
the flowers will bloom.

RE-THINK

I used to think -
to go to bed and sleep
without the finger of conscience
prodding me awake was worth
a hundred hours of wanton pleasure,
but a halo is uncomfortable to wear
when it grows tighter every year
and the days drag by
on leaden feet.

Maybe just a few hours of pleasure
would only warrant a gentle shake
and then
I could go back to sleep
warm and smiling -
reminiscing.

ST. JUST IN ROSELAND
Photo: Rosemary Arthur

THERE WILL COME A TIME

She said - "If I had known it would be like this
I would have told him I could be content with
just a fragment of his love, not that it must end
for I have lost my lover and my friend -
alone I am a puppet with no one to pull the strings,
a lifeless, useless thing, and memories shuttle
back and forth inside my head as loose bobbins
on a broken thread, and through the sadness
runs a streak of madness, a temporary insanity
clouding my reason, destroying all vanity.

"Before I can live again I must suffer pain
to justify my misery - battle with an overwhelming force,
face nature in its wild ferocity and accept
there can be no victory;
I feel the need to stand four-square against
the biting wind, let ice-cold shafts of sleet pierce my cheek,
and watch the fierce unrelenting tide crash on the shore
the waves clawing up the cliff as they rise and fall again
capturing my mood, echoing my pain, and let
the harsh spray fall as salt tears upon my skin
bitter as the hurt within.
"There will come a time when I shall laugh again,
and talk, and long for loving arms to hold me close,
but till then I must walk alone, my life bleak and empty,
bare of conversation, and I must wait patiently
for a sign that once more the will to live is mine
and filled with expectation, for life should move
in pairs, dancing to the rhythm of creation".

FOUR FACES OF SILENCE

Silence wears four faces, only two are smiling,
the others, masked, half concealed
wrapped in emotional power that wields unease,
nerve ends split, hearts wildly pound
begging for a friendly voice, a friendly sound.

Silence, solid to the touch, impenetrable;
blank as a wall, blunting fingers, breaking hearts,
unmindful of the tears that fall.

One happy face of silence symbolises solitude and peace,
in this strident world, how we long for noise to cease,
to hear the singing of the lark;
quiet waiting for the flame lit by a spark.

Everything is changed by love -
questing fingers in a silken glove -
and minds, tongued and grooved
needing few words, as actions proved;
this tender face of silence, so beguiling,
love warming it to softly smiling.

ANOTHER CLEOPATRA

She was not young, and certainly no beauty,
her charismatic radiance made the supermarket
a stage, the seried ranks of beans and tuna fish
her chorus, the shoppers a restless, changing audience
as people looked, then looked again, trying in vain
to define the mystery of female scorcery.

Old men gazed with wistful memory, turning away,
envious of youth and fulfilled dreams -
the young men, hope still burning, stared
with timeless desire, eager as impatient dogs
waiting for a sign to chase and retrieve
the thrown stick.

From a distance the women watched
wary of the eternal Eve,
ready to spit with venom tongue,
green demon's claws unsheath;
conscious of her power but feigning unconcern,
an enigmatic smile upon her face
she moved with sensuous grace -
another Cleopatra.

FALSE MOVE

It seemed a good idea to find a smaller place -
neat and modern, labour saving -
this house is all of that, but clinical and cold,
not where I could grow old gracefully,
everything is so impersonal - no lived-in atmosphere -
I feel it is almost an offence to cough.

Our old house had its faults
but it welcomed me with loving arms
and whispered to me softly through the landing window.
I miss the walk through tangled grass to the stones
where Tibby, Mr. Pusskin and old Hector lie,
half forgotten, with the growing pains of childhood.
We did not need the attic any more
but hopefully in a few years time there will be
another generation to fill it with their toys
or they might have done if we had stayed,
here there is no room for sentiment.

I have not transplanted very well,
my roots are bruised and torn and I am alien
in this too perfect sterile place
I miss the slipshod corners and the daisies on the lawn
and shall become stunted with no spontaneous joy
no wild flamboyant flowering,
the soil and everything around is antiseptic -
I shall struggle to survive, but I need
a slight touch of decadence before
I can bloom again.

REMORSE

The woman said to me -
"I crave for peace, above all, peace of mind -
if I could have just one gift
it would be serenity, for
regret and remorse tear into my soul
as a lion on a wounded calf -
eating it away.

"In middle age I live again my Mother's life,
see it through her eyes, with fear
of old age and loneliness,
the loss of independence, clarity of mind, mobility,
but most of all, the loss of friends
and of their company.

"I gave her grudging love and scant comfort,
my life was too full to fill her empty days -
always tomorrow would be the day I'd go and stay.
I grieve more now than on the day she died,
self-pity in a thin veiled gown,
as I plead leniency for my blindness to see her need,
and I regret I did not curb my impatience,
put a bridle on my hasty tongue and
walk with her on that lonely path,
and show a little love.
regret and remorse eat into my soul and
will not let me rest",
and as the woman walked away
there was an echo of her words in my own heart.

SAM'S PATCH
Photo: Rosemary Arthur

CORN DOLLY

When corn is green, it stands strong and stiff
as soldiers in a vast battalion
regimented by wind and rain, swaying in unison
to command of an unseen sergeant breathing instructions
to bow to every wind that blows.

When corn is gold it is less disciplined,
mellowed by warm sunny days, ears filled with
the hum of satiated bees, relaxed and so receptive
to many a laughing temptress as the poppy flaunts
her scarlet petticoats and flirts with wide open eyes,
living for a wild brief day, an open invitation
to dally awhile she is wanton in her choice of bedfellow
before sharp blades mingle the petals with the grain
for like the bold campfollowers of old
few can restrain the advances of
the poppies in the lane.

THE JACARANDA TREE

The young girl born in poverty
had an unexpected sensitivity,
she loathed the sordid inner city obscenities
but there was no escape, except in fantasy
and a talisman - the picture
of a Jacaranda tree.

She smiled as she walked by the callow, spotty youth
beside a stunted precinct tree,
she could no longer see
the desolated rain-shone square, the narrow littered street,
for there was an enchanted forest path
leading to a palm-fringed lake and
the gondola that would take her
to the handsome stranger who waited patiently
beneath a blue-flowered Jacaranda tree,
he would become her lover and for a brief while
she'd find romance, before the brutal world
would claim her back into the coarse arms
of reality.

COLOURFUL WORLD

Life is a rainbow of pink and blue and green and gold,
and finally, so beautiful to behold -
deep ruby red
which runs like a living thread
throughout our lives, and through our heart,
but, at the very start - life is pink -
with the dawn and a shell pink sky,
and the sound of a baby's cry, for a newborn babe
is soft and pink and warm, as delicate as a rosebud
until a child begins to form, and the blue of its eye
is likened to the sky,
and to the sea that ebbs and flows relentlessly.

Life is green - the colour of youth and innocence
until we gain experience, and it is
the colour of all growing things
of plants and flowers and trees - and Spring -
the basic carpet of the earth whose territory
is immense and shows nature in abundance.

Life is gold - a sign that many things are growing old,
for Autumn is burnished like corn's ripening ears
and the middle years,
a time when all is mellow and just a little sad,
a time for looking back over the life we've had.

Life turns to red, the colour of maturity
when the dying sun bids a glorious goodbye
with vivid streaks across the sky, pink and gold
and bright vermillion, pale coral and deep glowing crimson,
with a beauty that transcends all painter's art
and has warmed many a weary heart
like the heat of burning embers in the cold
of bleak Decembers, the perfect ending
and farewell to the sun, when all is peace
and day is done.

IMPOSSIBLE QUESTIONS

Why does it always rain just when my washing's dry
and when I've got a dreadful headache, the baby starts to cry?
why do visitors always call when I turn the cupboards out,
and I am tired and dirty and the toys are all about?
why do they never come when the house is shiny bright
and on a quiet evening, not on an interesting telly night.
why does my beloved forget to buy the wine
on the occasions the Boss and his wife come to dine?
and the champagne comes to a splutter when I have an empty glass,
and I often meet an obstruction just where another car wants to pass?

Why does the fattest person always sit by me on the bus
and it's only when I scrape the car my husband makes a fuss?
In the quiet of the church why do I often sneeze
and he wants Welsh rarebit when I forgot to buy the cheese?
why is there always a grating just where I drop the key,
and on the day I run out of cake, his Mother comes to tea?

Why is it always the *last* bus just disappearing out of sight,
and when the central heating fails, it is the coldest night?
Why does the cat chose to have kittens on the softest bed
and if there is a row, it is always something I have said?
and when I get a ladder in my tights it is always my last pair,
and I'm sure to meet someone special when I need to wash my hair?

Why do I ask so many questions that no one seems to know?
but I suppose I'll go on asking, till someone
tells me where to go!!

ESPECIALLY THE SMALL THINGS

I thank you Lord for so many things,
but especially the small things
that touch our heart for they convey
the wonder and miracle of life each day -
I love the glory of each flower that grows
the majestic lily and the perfect rose,
but also the scarlet poppy hiding in the corn,
the first snowdrop, and the daisy on the lawn
for they are brave survivors and return
to show us that we too can learn
to rise above the sorrow and the pain
to live and love and laugh again.

Thank you for the singing birds and
for the beauty of their wings,
but there is one I love to see that never sings,
the humble sparrow, dull and brown
hopping cheekily around when there are crumbs upon the ground.

I thank you for my home and for my garden
where the plants I've grown are living reminders
of the many friends I've known,
and thank you for my bed, a haven for my weary head,
I think maybe I love it best, for there I am
as warm and cosy as a fledgling in a nest, and
I thank you for the solace of sleep
to calm the mind and free me from the need to weep,
and for the company of family and friends
and the love that never ends,
but most of all, when I awake, I pray
and thank God for the coming day.